Dear Family,

What's the best way to help your child love reading?

Find good books like this one to share—and read together!

Here are some tips.

● **Take a "picture walk."** Look at all the pictures before you read. Talk about what you see.

● **Take turns.** Read to your child. Ham it up! Use different voices for different characters, and read with feeling! Then listen as your child reads to you, or explains the story in his or her own words.

● **Point out words as you read.** Help your child notice how letters and sounds go together. Point out unusual or difficult words that your child might not know. Talk about those words and what they mean.

● **Ask questions.** Stop to ask questions as you read. For example: "What do you think will happen next?" "How would you feel if that happened to you?"

● **Read every day.** Good stories are worth reading more than once! Read signs, labels, and even cereal boxes with your child. Visit the library to take out more books. And look for other JUST FOR YOU! BOOKS you and your child can share!

The Editors

For Ken, Alexis, and Olivia, and for Moms like no other—
Audrey, Ernestine, and Barb B.
—CTB

To Mom, Dad, and Samtra Devard:
Thank you for being so supportive!
—ND

Text copyright © 2004 by Christine Taylor-Butler.
Illustrations copyright © 2004 by Nancy Devard.
Produced for Scholastic by COLOR-BRIDGE BOOKS, LLC, Brooklyn, NY
All rights reserved. Published by SCHOLASTIC INC.
JUST FOR YOU! is a trademark of Scholastic Inc.

Library of Congress Cataloging-in-Publication Data

Taylor-Butler, Christine.
  A mom like no other / by Christine Taylor-Butler ; illustrated by Nancy Devard.
      p. cm.—(Just for you! Level 2)
  Summary: Despite their differences, an African American mother and daughter enjoy a special relationship.
      ISBN 0-439-56853-6 (pbk.)
      [1. Mothers and daughters—Fiction. 2. African Americans—Fiction. 3. Best friends—Fiction. 4. Friendship—Fiction. 5. Stories in rhyme.] I. Devard, Nancy, ill.
  II.Title. III. Series.
      PZ8.3.T2175Mo2004
      [E]—dc22   2004042910

10 9 8 7 6   08
            Printed in the U.S.A. 23 • First Scholastic Printing, February 2004

A Mom Like No Other

by Christine Taylor-Butler
Illustrated by Nancy Devard

My mother is cool.
She's more fun than she seems.

She is different than me,
but we make a good team.

I listen to rap music.
Mom dances to pop.

When we turn up the sound,
my dad begs us to stop.

My Mom adores soul food.
I like Chinese.

When she serves greens and cornbread,
I say, "Egg rolls, please!"

She wears a short Afro.
I have lots of braids.

I play in the sunlight.
She reads in the shade.

We're the best of best friends,
but I have a confession.

She's not my best friend
during corn-rowing sessions.

Mom makes her own clothes.
We buy mine at the mall.

She wears loud, bright colors.
I like pink, and that's all.

She's up before sunrise.
I'd rather sleep late.

So she tempts me with pancakes,
and I take the bait.

She's good with a hammer.

I'd rather use glue.

I love her new birdhouse.

What's mine? Not a clue!

Although we are different,
Mom knows what I like.

She straps on her skates
while I hop on my bike.

We no sooner start out,
than I fall; bang my chin.

She smiles, helps me up,
and says, "Try that again."

If a spider appears
Mom is scared as can be!

I pick it right up.
Spiders don't frighten me!

But when movies are scary,
I cover my eyes.

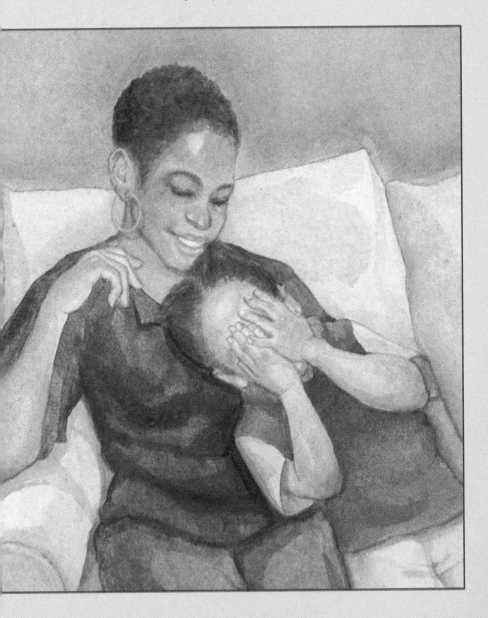

Mom says, "Girlfriend, please!
Those are fake dragonflies!"

I am not very patient.
She's funny and clever.

I give up on hard games.

Mom says, "Never say never."

She shows me there's nothing
that I can't achieve.

You just have to work hard,
and you have to believe.

Though we're different, it's clear
she's a friend like no other.

That's why I am glad
she is also my mother!

▲▲▲▲▲▲ JUST FOR YOU ▲▲▲

Here are some fun things for you to do.

What Do YOU Like?

The girl in the story
likes to eat pancakes.
She likes egg rolls, too!
What do YOU like to eat?

She likes to wear pink!
What color do YOU
like to wear?

She likes to ride
her bike.
What do YOU like
to do outside?

Write a story about
what YOU like!

Tell about your favorite
foods, colors, and what
you like to do.

You can draw pictures
to go with your story, too.

What Will YOU Achieve?

Achieve is a word that rhymes with believe. To achieve means to reach a goal, or make a dream come true.

The girl and her mom are wearing caps and gowns. What do you think they achieved?

Tell a friend about YOUR goals and dreams. What do YOU want to achieve? If you work hard and believe, you can do it!

▲▲▲TOGETHER TIME ▲▲▲▲

Make some time to share ideas about the story with your young reader! Here are some activities you can try. There are no right or wrong answers!

Read It Again: Clever rhymes make this story fun to read! Read it aloud as your child calls out the rhyming words. Maybe you two will want to try writing some rhymes together!

Think About It: Ask your child, "What do you think the girl's mother means when she says 'never say never'?" Can you two remember a time when your child said, "I'll never be able to do this!"? What happened?

Talk About It: The girl in the story says that she and her mom are different. Talk with your child about how you two are different. Talk about how you are alike. Make sure you share the things you like best about each other!

Meet the Author

CHRISTINE TAYLOR-BUTLER says, "When I was growing up, I had a special friend who was the total opposite of me. She played games with me, laughed with me, and hugged me during scary movies. We didn't always agree, but we were always there for each other. She showed me that I could do anything if I truly believed in myself. That person was my mom–and she is still my best friend!"

Christine spent most of her childhood with her head firmly planted in a book. She practically lived in the Cleveland Public Library in Ohio, where she grew up. She graduated from the Massachusetts Institute of Technology, and earned degrees in both Art & Design and Civil Engineering. Christine spent 11 years working for Hallmark Cards before becoming an author. Her first book in the JUST FOR YOU! series, *No Boys Allowed!*, was published in 2003. She lives in Kansas City, Missouri, with her husband, two daughters, and three cats.

Meet the Artist

NANCY DEVARD says, "I come from a family with two very creative parents, who always encouraged my brothers and me. I started drawing when I was three. My parents bought me real drawing pads and pencils. My dad challenged me to copy a portrait of him freehand, without tracing. I loved that challenge, worked hard, and practiced drawing from that point on. I get a very cool

feeling, and a real sense of pride, from looking at artwork I've created, and knowing, 'I made that!'"

Nancy is a graduate of Temple University and the Pennsylvania Academy of Fine Arts. She worked for more than six years as a staff artist for Hallmark Cards, and created many recognizable images for the Mahogany Cards division, which publishes African-American greeting cards. Nancy has exhibited her work in galleries on the East Coast and in the Midwest. This is her first children's book.